"To anybody who has ever lost control."
– Anabelle

"To my sweet little hurricane, Sofia."
– Martina

THIS BOOK BELONGS TO:

_____

MY FEELINGS ARE A HURRICANE

© 2021 Anabelle Wallick and Krystal Wallick. All rights reserved. No part of this book may be used or reproduced by any means, graphic, electronic or mechanical, including photocopying, recording, taping, or by any information storage retrieval system without the written permission of the publisher except in the case of brief quotations embodied in critical articles and reviews.

RAINBOW WINGS PUBLISHING LLC books are available from your favorite bookseller or from www.rainbowwingspublishing.com

Paperback ISBN: 978-1-7363828-9-9
Ebook ISBN: 978-1-7363828-8-2

Library of Congress Control Number: 2021915119
Cataloging in Publication data on file with the publisher.

Cover and Layout Design: Rachel Thomaier

Printed in the USA

10 9 8 7 6 5 4 3 2 1

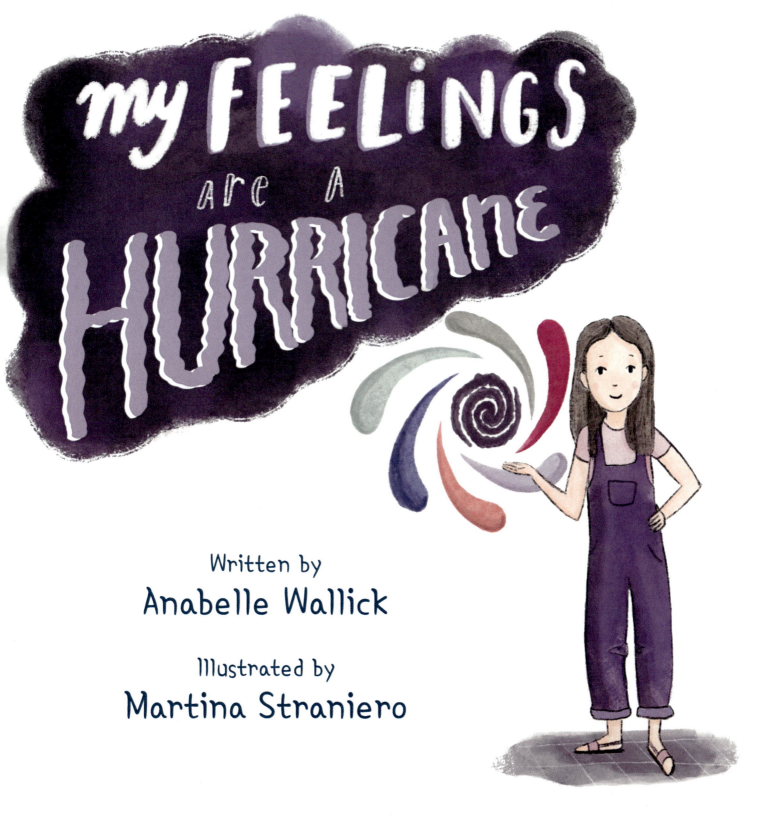

My feelings are a hurricane, but how can that be?

Feelings are not weather. Feelings are a part of me.

Sometimes, I feel AFRAID when I have to get a shot

or when I try something new. My stomach's in a knot!

Sometimes, all of those feelings happen at the same time. They begin to swirl together. They crash and collide.

Hurricanes occur when warm and cold air rise and spin.

That's exactly what it feels like deep inside my skin.

11

The SAD,
 the ANGRY,
  and the SCARED fight to be on top.

There's a battle going on.
I wish it would just STOP!

As my feelings swirl,

the hurricane gets much bigger.

I start to lose control

of all its

MIGHT and

VIGOR.

And SUDDENLY, the spinning gets me OUT OF CONTROL.

Just when I feel like there is no way to chill out

My brain reminds me that I'VE GOT THIS, no doubt!

Taking deep breaths can slow down the SPINNING and SWIRLING. It SLOWS DOWN my heart and helps me manage the whirling.

But how can I breathe deeply when I'm ANGRY and SAD?

I turn it into a game to get rid of the MAD.

I breathe in deeply through my nose while I twist my wrists.
Then I exhale the flow as I open up my fists.

3 release wrists
4 exhale

21

Pretzel breaths are also very relaxing to do.
I twist my arms tightly.
Through my nose, I inhale too.

I squeeze my arms like I am grabbing the hurricane. When I exhale, I let them loose to calm down my brain.

Deep breathing like this sends a signal up to my mind.

It tells my body that everything can unwind.

Then I start to feel the hurricane falling apart.
The happy creeps into my body and to my heart.

Together, my heart and my mind know just what to do.
They get my body in control
right from head to shoe.

Then, once my hurricane has totally disappeared, I can use my coping skills, and I'll stop feeling weird. I have lots of coping skills that help to keep me calm.

I like things like reading, drawing, or talking to Mom.
Or I talk to Grandma, Dad, or to one of my friends.
Or I play with a fidget toy that squishes and bends.

Do you ever think that your feelings are SWIRLING too?

And that there is a hurricane LURKING inside you?

You are not alone, you know. Sometimes, I feel it too. Take a deep breath, and very soon, you will feel brand new.

ABOUT THE AUTHOR

Anabelle Wallick is an elementary school student. She has always had a love of reading, writing, and drawing. One day after feeling particularly upset, she went to her room to draw her feelings. When she came out, she had drawn a picture of a hurricane filled with different facial expressions. This inspired her to turn her drawing into a book. She hopes that this story will help other children feel not so alone when they lose control of their emotions, as well as give them skills to be able to calm their body. Anabelle loves all things ice cream, rainbows, glitter, and unicorns. She lives in south Florida with her parents, two younger siblings, two dogs, and two cats.

ABOUT THE ILLUSTRATOR

Martina Straniero is an Italian architect and children's book illustrator currently living in Texas with her husband and her two little girls. She has always loved drawing and her dream of becoming an illustrator has finally come true. My Feelings Are A Hurricane is Martina's second children's book as illustrator.

You can find out more at linktr.ee/martinacartina.

Made in the USA
Columbia, SC
12 August 2022